Read & Respo
1

G000272640

Ages
5~7

Read & Respond

Ages
5–7

Author: Louise Carruthers

Commissioning Editor: Rachel Mackinnon

Editor: Tracy Kewely

Assistant Editor: Vicky Butt

Series Designer: Anna Oliwa

Designer: Liz Gilbert

Cover Image: Barbara Firth

Illustrations: Barbara Firth and Shelagh McNicolas

Text © 2010 Louise Carruthers © 2010 Scholastic Ltd

Designed using Adobe InDesign

Published by Scholastic Ltd, Book End,
Range Road, Witney,
Oxfordshire OX29 0YD
www.scholastic.co.uk

Printed by Bell & Bain
1 2 3 4 5 6 7 8 9   0 1 2 3 4 5 6 7 8 9

British Library Cataloguing-in-Publication Data
A catalogue record for this book is available from the British Library.

ISBN 978-1407-11899-4

The right of Louise Carruthers to be identified as the author of this work has been asserted by her in accordance with the Copyright, Designs and Patents Act 1988.

Extracts from Primary National Strategy's *Primary Framework for Literacy* (2006) http://nationalstrategies.standards.dcsf.gov.uk/primary/primaryframework/ © Crown copyright. Reproduced under the terms of Click Use Licence.

All rights reserved. This book is sold subject to the condition that it shall not, by way of trade or otherwise, be lent, hired out or otherwise circulated without the publisher's prior consent in any form of binding or cover other than that in which it is published and without a similar condition, including this condition, being imposed upon the subsequent purchaser.

No part of this publication may be reproduced, stored in a retrieval system, or transmitted, in any form or by any means, electronic, mechanical, photocopying, recording or otherwise, without the prior permission of the publisher. This book remains copyright, although permission is granted to copy pages where indicated for classroom distribution and use only in the school which has purchased the book, or by the teacher who has purchased the book, and in accordance with the CLA licensing agreement. Photocopying permission is given only for purchasers and not for borrowers of books from any lending service.

Acknowledgements

The publishers gratefully acknowledge permission to reproduce the following copyright material: **Walker Books** for the use of extracts, illustrations and the cover from *Can't You Sleep, Little Bear?* by Martin Waddell. Text © 1988, Martin Waddell. Illustrations © 1988 Barbara Firth (1988, Walker Books).
Every effort has been made to trace copyright holders for the works reproduced in this book, and the publishers apologise for any inadvertent omissions.

PAGE
2

READ & RESPOND: Activities based on Can't You Sleep, Little Bear?

Can't You Sleep, Little Bear?

About the book

Can't You Sleep, Little Bear? is a charming story about two bears, Big Bear and Little Bear. After a busy day playing in the snow, the bears return home to their cave. Big Bear puts Little Bear to bed before settling down by the fire to read his Bear Book. Little Bear is afraid of the dark and can't sleep, so Big Bear lights a tiny lantern and puts it next to Little Bear's bed. But Little Bear is still afraid, even when Big Bear brings out bigger and bigger lanterns. Even the 'Biggest Lantern of Them All' cannot light up the dark outside! Eventually, Big Bear finds a way to reassure Little Bear, leaving Big Bear to get on with finishing his Bear Book at last.

Can't You Sleep, Little Bear? is a good example of a story with predictable and patterned language and a wonderful starting point from which to develop children's literacy skills through a variety of speaking and listening, drama, reading and writing activities. Young children will be able to draw on their own experiences of bedtime and feeling afraid when exploring the themes and issues raised by the text. The book has detailed watercolour illustrations that support the narrative and bring the setting and characters to life.

About the author

Martin Waddell was born on the 10 April 1941 in the midst of a bombing raid on Belfast during the Second World War. Married, with three grown-up children, he has lived close to the Mountains of Mourne in County Down for most of his life and many of his stories have been inspired by events that have happened to him here. Martin wrote books for adults and teenagers before writing his first book for younger children, *Blue Velvet Dress*, in 1972. Since then, he has written many well-known picture books for children, including the *Little Bear* series, *Owl Babies* and *The Pig in the Pond*. Two times winner of the Smarties Book Prize for *Can't You Sleep, Little Bear?* and *Farmer Duck*, Martin also won the Kurt Maschler Award for *The Park in the Dark* and the Best Books for Babies Award for *Rosie's Babies*. In 2004, Martin Waddell was awarded the Hans Christian Andersen Author Award in recognition of his outstanding contribution to children's literature.

About the illustrator

Barbara Firth has been interested in drawing for as long as she can remember and began drawing plants and animals at the age of three. She studied pattern cutting at the London College of Fashion and worked for the knitting books division of *Vogue*, producing step-by-step illustrations of knitting, crocheting and dressmaking. It was with Walker Books that she began to do illustration work in her favourite field, natural history, and has gone on to illustrate many award-winning books. She now lives in Harrow, England.

Facts and figures
Can't You Sleep, Little Bear?
Author: Martin Waddell
Illustrator: Barbara Firth
First published: 1988 by Walker Books
Awards: The Smarties Book Prize (1988) and the Kate Greenaway Medal (1988).
Can't You Sleep, Little Bear? was the first in a series of *Little Bear* books, all published by Walker Books. Other titles in the series are: *Let's Go Home, Little Bear; You and Me, Little Bear; Well Done, Little Bear* and *Sleep Tight, Little Bear*. More than 7 million *Little Bear* books have been sold worldwide.

PAGE 3

READ & RESPOND: Activities based on Can't You Sleep, Little Bear?

Guided reading

The cover

Show the children the front cover of *Can't You Sleep, Little Bear?* Talk about the cover illustration. Encourage the children to make predictions about the story setting, characters and plot. Pose simple questions such as: *Do you think the bear in the picture will be the main character in the story? What is he doing? Where do you think the story is set? Is it daytime or night-time? How do you know? What other characters do you think might be in the story? What do you think will happen?*

Ask the children to locate and read the title of the story. Notice that the title is a question. Speculate who might be asking the question, for example Little Bear's mother or father. Consider what might be keeping Little Bear awake (a clock ticking, a thunderstorm and so on). Have any of the children ever had difficulty sleeping? What did they do? Read the text at the foot of the front cover. Discuss the roles of Martin Waddell and Barbara Firth using the terms 'author' and 'illustrator'. Ask: *Have you heard either of these names before? Have you read any other books written by Martin Waddell? What were they about?*

The back cover

Turn to the back cover of the book and read the blurb with the children to give them an idea of what the story is going to be about. Draw attention to how the blurb summarises the story without giving everything away. Explore any other information that has been included on the back cover of your version of the book (for example, quotes from reviews, information about other titles in the *Little Bear* series). Consider the purpose of this information.

Encourage the children to use the information given in the blurb to make further predictions about what might happen in the story. Ask: *What do you think Big Bear does to help Little Bear fall asleep?*

Point out the Walker Books logo on the back cover. Ask: *Have you seen this symbol before? What does it tell the reader? Can you remember the names of any other Walker Books we have read?*

First reading

Throughout the first reading of the story, model fluent, expressive reading. Encourage the children to join in with the repeated phrases as these become familiar. Spend time exploring the detailed illustrations that help to bring the story to life. Pause at significant points in the story to allow the children to share their personal responses to the text. Encourage them to predict what is going to happen next based on their understanding of ideas, characters and events. Pose questions such as: *Why do you think Little Bear can't get to sleep? Do you think Big Bear will be able to finish his Bear Book this time? Why not? What do you think Big Bear will do next to try to help Little Bear overcome his fear of the darkness?*

After the first reading of the text, spend time discussing the children's responses to the story. Ask them to identify aspects of the story that they particularly liked or disliked and encourage them to make links between the story and their personal experiences of being afraid of the dark or being unable to sleep.

Subsequent readings

In subsequent readings of the text it is important to reinforce, practise and develop key reading skills such as left to right directionality, one-to-one correspondence, decoding strategies, high frequency word recognition, vocabulary expansion and comprehension skills. Outlined below are some suggestions for using *Can't You Sleep, Little Bear?* to develop these key reading strategies.

Before each reading of the text, it is essential to establish the primary focus of the session (for example, developing decoding skills) and the specific learning objectives that will be addressed. The focus should be determined by the needs and ability of the children in the group.

At the beginning of each guided reading session, take a few moments to review some

PAGE

4

READ & RESPOND: Activities based on Can't You Sleep, Little Bear?

of the reading strategies that the children have been taught, for example, phonics, context cues, word recognition and grammatical knowledge. As the children read, encourage them to apply these strategies independently and to self-correct mistakes.

On a snowy day

Read the story up to *But Little Bear couldn't get to sleep*, encouraging the children to join in. Discuss the story setting and characters. Ask: *Where do the bears live?* (A cave in a forest.) *What time of year do you think it is? Why? What do you think the bears like to do and eat? How do you know?* Using their knowledge of the story setting, encourage the children to speculate on what types of games the bears have been playing in the forest all day (snowball fights, hide and seek – keep a record of the children's ideas for a later activity). Discuss whether the children think this is an effective story opening. Does it make them want to read on? Why? What do they think is going to happen in the story?

Feeling afraid

Continue reading to the end of the following page (up to *"The dark all around us," said Little Bear*) modelling how to read the text with appropriate expression. Ask the children why they think Little Bear is scared of the dark. Ask: *Can the dark hurt you? Why not?*

Draw attention to the use of brackets in the first sentence. Explain that the author has used the brackets to enclose some of the text as an aside. Re-read the sentence, omitting the bracketed text. Does the sentence still make sense? Ask the children to say which version they prefer and why.

Read on to the end of the next page (up to *...by the light of the fire*) and explore the accompanying illustration. Identify the adjectives that have been used to describe the lantern (*tiny, tiniest*) and ask the children to suggest alternatives. Why do the children think Big Bear chose to light such a tiny lantern?

Underline the phrase *cuddling up in the glow* and ask the children to infer from this how the tiny light is making Little Bear feel (cosy, safe, reassured). Can they suggest an alternative phrase? (For example, snuggled up in the tiny light.)

Little Bear can't sleep

Read the next three spreads beginning *Little Bear tried to go to sleep...* and ending *...by the light of the fire*, after Big Bear has hung up the Biggest Lantern of Them All. Identify and underline the repeated phrases spoken by each character and discuss the effect of these on the reader. Draw attention to devices that indicate how the text should be read, including speech marks, question marks, exclamation marks and vocabulary (*yawned, asked*).

Consider the feelings, motives and behaviour of each bear. Look at the picture of Little Bear doing handstands on the bed. Do the children think Little Bear is really feeling scared?

Underline the phrase *the Biggest Lantern of Them All*. Ask the children to suggest alternative words and phrases to describe the lantern (for example gigantic, the biggest lantern in the world and so on).

Big Bear can't read his book

Turn to the next page, beginning *Little Bear tried and tried...* Look at the illustration. Do the children think Little Bear is really trying to go to sleep? Why not? Help the children to empathise with the way Big Bear is feeling by asking them to imagine how they would feel if someone disturbed them when they were trying to finish a good book or watch their favourite television programme. Ask: *What would you do/ say? How would you feel?* Identify the word used in the text to show the reader that Big Bear is feeling fed up (*groaned*). Ask the children to imagine themselves in Big Bear's situation. Do they think they would have been so patient? How might they have behaved differently?

Guided reading

The dark night

Read the next three spreads from *"I'm scared," said Little Bear* to *And Little Bear looked*. Model appropriate intonation and expression, for example by emphasising the raised intonation at the end of each question and by leaving a short pause after the ellipsis. Invite the children to explain in their own words what Big Bear has done (taken Little Bear outside into the darkness). Do the children think this is a good idea? Why/why not? Highlight the word *DARK*. Discuss why Martin Waddell has written the word in capital letters. Ask: *Why does the author want to make this word stand out? What type of voice should be used when saying this word? What else has the author used to tell the reader to put emphasis on this word?* (An exclamation mark.) Speculate on how the bears are feeling. Why does Little Bear cuddle up to Big Bear?

Asleep at last

Read on to the end of the story. Ask the children to describe in their own words how Big Bear finally manages to get Little Bear to sleep. Consider the contented expressions on both of the bears' faces. Discuss how Big Bear must be feeling now he can finally sit down by the fire and get on with finishing his Bear Book (pleased, relieved and so on). Ask the children to suggest what they think Big Bear might be thinking, for example: *Finally, I can get on and finish my book in peace!*

Invite the children to give their opinions about the story. Which part of the story did they like best? Who was their favourite character? Why? Identify and discuss themes raised by the story (not being able to sleep, fear of the dark, caring) and encourage the children to relate these issues to their own experience.

PAGE
6

READ & RESPOND: Activities based on Can't You Sleep, Little Bear?

Shared reading

Extract 1

- Read an enlarged copy of Extract 1 together, encouraging the children to apply their phonic knowledge and skills to decode unknown words.
- Working together, circle all of the words in the extract that contain the phoneme /air/ (*bear, there, scared, chair*).
- Ask the children to underline the grapheme that represents the /air/ sound in each of the words.
- Generate lists of other words that contain the graphemes 'air', 'are', 'ear' on the board.
- Explore the different ways in which capital letters are used in the text. Remind the children that capital letters are used at the beginning of sentences, and circle the relevant words on the extract.
- Ask the children to look for other words in the extract that have capital letters (for example, *Little Bear, Lantern Cupboard, Bear Book*). Discuss with the children why they think these words start with capital letters.

Extract 2

- Read an enlarged copy of Extract 2.
- Talk about the purpose of speech marks. Help the children to circle all of the speech marks and then underline all of the direct speech, using a different colour for each character.
- Ask the children to say how they know which character is speaking when (*said Little Bear, asked Big Bear* and so on). Highlight the word *grunted* on the extract. Ask: *What does this word tell us about how Big Bear is feeling?* (Fed up, annoyed.) *Why is he feeling fed up? What clues does this word give us about how the dialogue should be read?*
- Invite the children to suggest appropriate alternatives that could be used as substitutions for the word *said* throughout the extract, to give more detail about how each character is speaking (for example cried, sighed). Annotate the text with the children's suggestions.
- Divide the class into two groups and re-read the extract, with one group reading the dialogue spoken by Big Bear and the other group the dialogue spoken by Little Bear.

Extract 3

- Read an enlarged copy of Extract 3 at a good pace, modelling appropriate expression and intonation.
- Explore the way in which text has been presented. Ask: *Why has the word DARK been written in upper case bold lettering?* (To give emphasis to the word.) *How does this influence the way we say the word when reading the text? How does this make the reader feel? What else has the author used to give emphasis to this and other words in the extract?* (An exclamation mark.)
- Underline the adjectives *bright, yellow* and *twinkly* on the text extract. Recap the purpose of adjectives: they describe nouns (in this case *moon* and *stars*) and help to make a piece of writing more interesting.
- Ask the children to think of other adjectives that could be used to describe the moon and stars. Compile a list of their suggestions.
- Invite volunteers to read the final sentence on the extract, substituting the three adjectives for alternatives from the list on the board.

Extract 1

Big Bear looked, and he saw that the dark part of the cave was very dark, so he went to the Lantern Cupboard and took out the tiniest lantern that was there.

Big Bear lit the tiniest lantern, and put it near to Little Bear's bed.

"There's a tiny light to stop you being scared, Little Bear," said Big Bear.

"Thank you, Big Bear," said Little Bear, cuddling up in the glow.

"Now go to sleep, Little Bear," said Big Bear, and he padded back to the Bear Chair and settled down to read the Bear Book, by the light of the fire.

Text © 1988, Martin Waddell; illustration © 1988, Barbara Firth.

PHOTOCOPIABLE

PAGE
8

SCHOLASTIC
www.scholastic.co.uk

READ & RESPOND: Activities based on Can't You Sleep, Little Bear?

Extract 2

"Can't you sleep, Little Bear?" grunted Big Bear, putting down his Bear Book (with just three pages to go) and padding over to the bed.

"I'm scared," said Little Bear.

"Why are you scared, Little Bear?" asked Big Bear.

"I don't like the dark," said Little Bear.

"What dark?" asked Big Bear.

"The dark all around us," said Little Bear.

"But I brought you two lanterns!" said Big Bear. "A tiny one and a bigger one!"

"Not much bigger," said Little Bear. "And there's still lots of dark."

Text © 1988, Martin Waddell; illustration © 1988, Barbara Firth.

SCHOLASTIC
www.scholastic.co.uk

PAGE 9

PHOTOCOPIABLE

READ & RESPOND: Activities based on Can't You Sleep, Little Bear?

Extract 3

DARK!

"Ooooh! I'm scared," said Little Bear, cuddling up to Big Bear.

Big Bear lifted Little Bear, and cuddled him, and said, "Look at the dark, Little Bear." And Little Bear looked.

"I've brought you the moon, Little Bear," said Big Bear. "The bright yellow moon, and all the twinkly stars."

PHOTOCOPIABLE

READ & RESPOND: Activities based on Can't You Sleep, Little Bear?

SCHOLASTIC
www.scholastic.co.uk

Text © 1988, Martin Waddell; illustration © 1988, Barbara Firth.

Plot, character and setting

Big Bear and Little Bear

Objective: To give some reasons why things happen or characters change.
What you need: Copies of *Can't You Sleep, Little Bear?*, an enlarged set of the word cards on photocopiable page 15, paper and writing materials.
Cross-curricular link: PSHE.

What to do
● Ask the children to name the characters in *Can't You Sleep, Little Bear?*
● Read the story together, encouraging the children to consider the feelings, thoughts and actions of the two characters at different points in the story.
● Draw two bear shapes on the board – one big and one small.
● Hold up one of the word cards from photocopiable page 15 and ask the children to decide whether the word describes Big Bear or

Little Bear. (Note: some of the words could be used to describe both.) Encourage the children to locate evidence in the text and/or illustrations to support their decision. For example: *Little Bear was tired because he had been playing outside all day.* Let one of the children stick the word card onto the correct character shape.
● Repeat the activity using all of the cards.
● Give out paper and writing materials. Ask the children to draw a picture and write a simple description of one of the characters, using the adjectives on the board to help them.

Differentiation
For older/more confident learners: Challenge children to think of other adjectives to describe Big Bear and Little Bear.
For younger/less confident learners: Provide sentence starters for the children to complete. (For example: *Little Bear was tired because...*)

What the bears say

Objective: To explore familiar themes and characters through improvisation and role play.
What you need: Copies of *Can't You Sleep, Little Bear?*, two paper speech bubbles for each pair, writing materials.
Cross-curricular link: Drama.

What to do
● Turn to the page where Big Bear first visits Little Bear in his bed (beginning *"Can't you sleep, Little Bear?"*). Encourage the children to look at the illustration as you read the dialogue with appropriate intonation and expression (for example, a gentle, reassuring tone for Big Bear).
● Stop reading at the end of the page and organise the children into pairs. Ask them to continue the conversation in role as the characters in the story.
● Encourage the children to mirror the body language of the bears and to speak with

appropriate expression. (You may find it helpful to model the activity with an LSA first.)
● Repeat the activity using other illustrations, for example, the bears standing in the snow at the beginning of the book.
● Hand out two speech bubbles to each pair of children. Ask the children to use the speech bubbles to record one thing each bear said in their improvised conversation.
● Invite volunteers to share their work. Encourage the rest of the group to guess which bear is speaking and at which point in the story. How do they know?

Differentiation
For older/more confident learners: Ask children to write a longer dialogue using speech marks to demarcate direct speech.
For younger/less confident learners: Record children's dialogues on a Dictaphone or video recorder.

READ & RESPOND: Activities based on Can't You Sleep, Little Bear?

Plot, character and setting

Setting explorer

> **Objective:** To listen to others in class, ask relevant questions and follow instructions.
> **What you need:** Copies of *Can't You Sleep, Little Bear?*, pictures of caves.
> **Cross-curricular links:** Drama, geography.

What to do
● Referring to the illustrations in *Can't You Sleep, Little Bear?*, discuss the story setting (a cave in a snowy forest) with the children.
● Show the group some cave pictures. Ask: *What is a cave? Have you ever seen/been inside a cave? What was it like?*
● Take the class into the hall. Using simple drama techniques, encourage the children to use all of their senses to explore an imaginary cave setting. Say, for example: *Imagine you are walking along a narrow winding path through a snowy forest. Suddenly the path disappears. You are standing in front of a cave. You go inside. Take care, the cave is dark and the roof low...*
● Tell the children to explore the cave. Say: *Touch the wall of the cave – how does it feel? It is dark and you stumble over something – what is it? You hear something moving, what could it be? How do you feel?*
● Sit in a circle. Invite each child to describe what they saw and heard and how they felt inside the cave. Encourage the children to ask each other relevant questions to find out more information.

> **Differentiation**
> **For older/more confident learners:** Encourage children to write a detailed description of an imaginary cave setting using adventurous word and language choices.
> **For younger/less confident learners:** Ask children to draw a picture of a cave setting and then describe their picture to a partner.

Who lives here?

> **Objective:** To explain ideas using imaginative and adventurous vocabulary.
> **What you need:** Copies of *Can't You Sleep, Little Bear?*, a collection of other stories that feature a cave as part of the setting (such as 'Aladdin', *We're Going on a Bear Hunt* by Michael Rosen, *We're Going on a Dragon Hunt* by Maurice Jones), a picture of a cave, photocopiable page 16.
> **Cross-curricular link:** Art and design.

What to do
● Explore a selection of stories that include a cave setting (see above). Ask the children to name any other stories they have read or watched that feature caves.
● Ask the children to suggest what sort of characters they might find in a cave setting (for example, a dragon, a witch, a monster). Record the children's ideas on the board. Talk about each suggested character in turn. Are they nice or nasty? What do they look like? How do they behave?
● Display a picture of a cave on the board. Tell the children to close their eyes and visualise who (or what!) lives inside the cave. Invite each child to describe their character (appearance, qualities and behaviour) to a talking partner.
● Hand out copies of photocopiable page 16. Ask each child to create a simple profile of their imaginary character.
● In a subsequent lesson, ask the children to plan and write a story featuring the cave-dwelling character they have created.

> **Differentiation**
> **For older/more confident learners:** Show the children how to use a thesaurus to make interesting word choices.
> **For younger/less confident learners:** Organise the children to work in mixed-ability pairs.

Plot, character and setting

On a snowy day

> **Objective:** To compose and write simple sentences independently to communicate meaning.
> **What you need:** Copies of *Can't You Sleep, Little Bear?*, an enlarged copy of photocopiable page 17 and a copy for each child, writing materials.

What to do

● Read the first two spreads of *Can't You Sleep, Little Bear?* (up to *But Little Bear couldn't get to sleep*). Pose simple questions about the story setting and main characters, for example: *Do the bears live in the town or the country? What time of year do you think it is? How do you know?*
● Highlight the sentence *They played all day in the bright sunlight.* Tell the children that you would like them to write a new opening for the story that includes more detail about the games Little Bear and Big Bear played.
● Refer back to your discussion from the guided

reading session about what games the bears may have played in the snow. Remind the children of the ideas they had and invite further ideas now.
● In shared writing, use some of the children's ideas to write a new opening for the story using the writing frame on photocopiable page 17.
● Give out copies of photocopiable page 17 for the children to complete independently.
● Let each child read out their story opening and vote for the class favourite. Re-read the shared text with the new opening.

> **Differentiation**
> **For older/more confident learners:** Expect the use of more complex sentences and adventurous vocabulary.
> **For younger/less confident learners:** Provide a word bank of relevant words and phrases to support writing.

Can't you...Little Bear?

> **Objective:** To explore familiar themes and characters through improvisation and role play.
> **What you need:** Copies of *Can't You Sleep, Little Bear?*, individual whiteboards and pens, a digital camera.
> **Cross-curricular link:** ICT.

What to do

● Tell the children that in this lesson they are going to plan and write a class story. Explain that the story is going to use the same story setting and characters as *Can't You Sleep, Little Bear?* but the plot (what happens) will be different.
● Write *Can't You...Little Bear?* on the board. Ask the children to think of a word or words that could be inserted into the gap to create a title for a new story (for example: *tie your laces, find your teddy*).
● Choose one of the ideas suggested by the

children to develop into a class story, for example, *Can't You Find Your Way Home, Little Bear?* Use improvisation and role play to develop imaginative ideas. Take photographs of the role play to record the main events in the story.
● Working as a class, sequence some or all of the digital photographs to create a story plan. Organise the children into pairs and give out whiteboards and pens. In shared writing, demonstrate how to write a simple story based on the class role play. Encourage the children to contribute ideas on their whiteboards.

> **Differentiation**
> **For older/more confident learners:** Ask children to write an extended narrative based on the class role play.
> **For younger/less confident learners:** Sequence three photographs and ask the children to write a simple sentence after each picture to tell a story.

Plot, character and setting

Paw prints

> **Objective:** To recognise the main elements that shape different texts.
> **What you need:** Copies of *Can't You Sleep, Little Bear?*, sheets of A3 paper with three large paw prints drawn on each sheet (one per pair).
> **Cross-curricular link:** Art and design.

What to do

● Read *Can't You Sleep, Little Bear?* Talk about the main incidents in the story and consider how the events are connected.
● Draw three giant bear paw prints on the board. Explain that each paw print represents a section of the story. Label the paw prints *Beginning*, *Middle* and *End*.
● Ask the children to recall what happens at the beginning of the story. (The bears play in the snow, then go back to their cave. Little Bear goes to bed. Big Bear reads his book.) Draw pictures to represent these events in the first paw print (for example snow, a cave, a book and a bed).
● Discuss the events that occur in the middle and at the end of the story and record these in pictures on the relevant paw prints.
● Hand out the sheets of A3 paper and ask the children in pairs to draw their own pictures on the paw prints to represent the events that occur at the beginning, middle and end of the story. Invite each pair to retell the story, using their paw prints to help them order the events.

> **Differentiation**
> **For older/more confident learners:** Ask the children to choose one of their paw prints and write this section of the story.
> **For younger/less confident learners:** Repeat the group activity with other stories that the children know well.

Retell the story

> **Objective:** To retell stories ordering events using story language.
> **What you need:** Photocopiable page 18.
> **Cross-curricular link:** Maths.

What to do

● Ask the children to recall the key events of *Can't You Sleep, Little Bear?* in the order in which they occur. Use careful questioning to encourage the children to use vocabulary related to sequence and time. For example: *What happened at the beginning of the story? What happened next? What did Big Bear do after Little Bear had fallen asleep?*
● Display a set of time connective cards from photocopiable page 18 on the board. Read the words aloud with the children and discuss their meaning.
● Organise the children to work in pairs. Give each pair their own set of time connective cards and ask them to hold up the connective they think would be the most suitable to use at the beginning or end of a story. Why do they think this?
● Ask the children to retell *Can't You Sleep, Little Bear?* to a partner, using the time connectives on photocopiable page 18 to link events.
● Invite several children to retell the story to the class. Instruct the rest of the group to listen carefully and signal each time they hear a time connective.

> **Differentiation**
> **For older/more confident learners:** Encourage the children to use phrases from the story when retelling the story.
> **For younger/less confident learners:** Let the children use the paw prints from the previous activity to remind them of the story structure but encourage them to use connectives in their retelling.

Big Bear and Little Bear

● Read the words below and decide if they describe Big Bear or Little Bear.

fed up	little
scared	patient
brave	tired
kind	big
clever	nervous

SCHOLASTIC
www.scholastic.co.uk

PAGE
15

PHOTOCOPIABLE

READ & RESPOND: Activities based on Can't You Sleep, Little Bear?

Plot, character and setting

Who lives here?

● Draw a picture of the person or creature you think might live in this cave.

Are they nice or nasty?

Think of words and phrases to describe what the person or creature looks like and what sort of character they are.

Illustration © 2010, Shelagh McNicolas.

Plot, character and setting

On a snowy day

● Write a new story opening for *Can't You Sleep, Little Bear?*

Big Bear and Little Bear played in the snow all day.

_____

_____

_____

_____

_____

_____

_____

When night came, they went home to the Bear Cave...

Illustration © 1988, Barbara Firth.

READ & RESPOND: Activities based on *Can't You Sleep, Little Bear?*

Plot, character and setting

Retell the story

● Use the words below to help you retell the story of *Can't You Sleep, Little Bear?*

after that	when night came
then	eventually
once	a few moments later
finally	next

READ & RESPOND: Activities based on *Can't You Sleep, Little Bear?*

Talk about it

Feeling scared

Objective: To tell stories and describe incidents from their own experience in an audible voice.
What you need: Copies of *Can't You Sleep, Little Bear?*, photocopiable page 22.
Cross-curricular link: PSHE.

What to do

● Turn to the ninth spread in the book that begins, *"I'm scared," said Little Bear.* Look at the illustration and read the text with appropriate expression. Ask the children to describe how Little Bear is feeling (scared) and why (he is afraid of the dark).
● Highlight the word *scared* on the text. Working in pairs, ask the children to think of synonyms for the word *scared* (frightened, terrified, worried and so on). Compile a word bank on the board.

● Ask the children to recall an occasion when they felt scared (for example, lost in a supermarket, first day at a new school). Let each child recount their experience to the group, encourage them to include details about when and where the incident took place, what happened and how they felt.
● Give each child photocopiable page 22 and ask them to plan and then write about a recount of experience they have shared with the group.

Differentiation
For older/more confident learners: Encourage the children to incorporate some of the synonyms contained in the word bank into both their oral and written recount.
For younger/less confident learners: Let children illustrate a simple story board to record their experience.

Role plays

Objective: To present their own stories for members of their own class.
What you need: Copies of *Can't You Sleep, Little Bear?*, photocopiable page 23.
Cross-curricular links: PSHE, citizenship, drama.

What to do

● Turn to the page in the story that begins *Big Bear put Little Bear to bed in the dark part of the cave.* Read the text on this page together.
● Ask the children to recall why Little Bear couldn't sleep. (He was scared of the dark.) Find out if any of the children are scared of the dark. If so, what is it about the dark that makes them feel afraid?
● Drawing on their own experiences, ask the children to suggest other things that might keep someone awake at night. (For example: loud

music, a dog barking, worrying about a test, a bad dream.) Record some of the children's suggestions on the board.
● Give each pair a copy of photocopiable page 23 and ask them to complete the activity orally. Discuss and compare the children's answers as a class.
● Ask each pair to devise a short role play about a child who couldn't sleep based on one of the images on photocopiable page 23. Let each pair present their role play to the rest of the class.

Differentiation
For older/more confident learners: Show the children how to record their role play in the form of a playscript.
For younger/less confident learners: Provide adult support during the paired activity.

Talk about it

I can't sleep!

> **Objective:** To explain their views to others in a small group and decide how to report the group's views to the class.
> **What you need:** Copies of *Can't You Sleep, Little Bear?*, individual whiteboards and pens.
> **Cross-curricular link:** PSHE.

What to do

● Read the first two spreads of *Can't You Sleep, Little Bear?* as far as *But Little Bear couldn't get to sleep*. Ask the children to recall why Little Bear was unable to get to sleep and discuss the different things Big Bear did to help him get to sleep.

● Organise the children into small groups of three or four. Ask the children to discuss what they do if they are having trouble sleeping. What sort of things do they do to help them get to sleep? (For example, read a book, have a drink of warm milk.) Where do they go? (Their parents' bedroom, downstairs.) Who do they ask for help? (Mum, dad, big brother.)

● Provide whiteboards and pens and nominate a scribe in each group to record the children's ideas.

● Finally, give each group the opportunity to report back the main points of their discussion to the rest of the class. Make a list of all the different strategies the children use to help them when they are having difficulty getting to sleep.

> **Differentiation**
> **For older/more confident learners:** Ask the children to write a letter to Big Bear suggesting other things he could do to help Little Bear get to sleep.
> **For younger/less confident learners:** Help the children to dramatise one of their experiences as a short role play.

Design a bedroom

> **Objective:** To listen to each other's views and preferences, agree the next steps to take and identify contributions by each group member.
> **What you need:** Copies of *Can't You Sleep, Little Bear?*, large sheets of paper, writing and drawing materials.

What to do

● Re-read the first two spreads of *Can't You Sleep, Little Bear?* Ask: *Why do you think Big Bear put Little Bear to sleep in the dark part of the cave? Would you like to sleep here? Why/why not?*

● Invite the children to describe their own bedrooms. What sort of things do they have in there? How do they feel when they get into bed? (For example, safe, cosy.)

● Explain that you would like the children to enter a competition to design a new bedroom for Little Bear. Ask them to work in small groups to plan, draw and label a bedroom for Little Bear. Encourage them to use their knowledge of the character when deciding what features to include. (For example, a nightlight, curtains to keep out the dark, wallpaper decorated with the moon and stars and so on.) Keep the children's designs for a writing activity (see page 27).

● Finally, let each group share their design with the rest of the class. Give the children an opportunity to express their views about each design before voting to decide the winner.

> **Differentiation**
> **For older/more confident learners:** Challenge children to write a description of the bedroom in the style of estate agents' particulars.
> **For younger/less confident learners:** Arrange for the children to work in a small group with an adult to support writing.

PAGE 20

READ & RESPOND: Activities based on Can't You Sleep, Little Bear?

Talk about it

A helping hand

> **Objective:** To explore familiar themes and characters through improvisation and role play.
> **What you need:** Copies of *Can't You Sleep, Little Bear?*, photocopiable page 24.
> **Cross-curricular link:** PSHE.

What to do

● Explore the relationship between the two characters in *Can't You Sleep, Little Bear?* Ask the children to describe some of the different ways in which Big Bear helps Little Bear in the story (puts him to bed, comforts him when he cannot sleep). Elicit that Big Bear is a very caring bear. Talk about how this is demonstrated in his words and actions.

● In circle time, invite each child to describe an incident when they needed help. What happened? Who helped them? (For example, a parent, carer, teacher or older sibling.) What did they do/say?

● Organise the children into groups of three or four. Give each group a role-play card from photocopiable page 24 and ask them to devise a short play based on the scenario set on the card. Encourage the children to pay particular attention to their body language, what they say and how they speak.

● Let each group perform their role play to the rest of the class. Discuss and evaluate each performance. Swap cards and repeat the activity.

> **Differentiation**
> **For older/more confident learners:** Encourage the children to suggest other suitable role-play scenarios.
> **For younger/less confident learners:** Ask the children in pairs to role play different parts of the story.

Selling the story

> **Objective:** To ensure that everyone contributes, allocate tasks, consider alternatives and reach agreement.
> **What you need:** Copies of *Can't You Sleep, Little Bear?*, individual whiteboards and pens, large sheets of paper, writing materials.
> **Cross-curricular links:** Art and design, ICT.

What to do

● Read the blurb on the back of *Can't You Sleep, Little Bear?* Ask the children to say whether the blurb makes them want to read the story. Why?

● Invite the children to share their opinions about the book. Ask questions such as: *Which part of the story do you like best? Why? Is there anything you don't like about the story? What do you think of the illustrations?*

● Organise the children into groups of three or four. Explain that you would like each group to design a poster to advertise the book that includes an attention-grabbing heading, information about the story and eye-catching illustrations.

● Emphasise that the purpose of the poster is to make people buy the book, and so it important to use positive descriptions and persuasive language.

● Make a list of ideas on the board (beautiful illustrations, happy ending, a brilliant book and so on).

● Give each group a sheet of paper and writing materials and ask them to design their poster. Monitor the groups carefully to enable every child to contribute to the task.

> **Differentiation**
> **For older/more confident learners:** Ask the children to design a poster that appeals to a particular target market (such as, parents choosing a bedtime story to read to their child, teachers).
> **For younger/less confident learners:** Ask the children to make a TV commercial to advertise the book.

SECTION 5

Feeling scared

● Little Bear was scared of the dark. Write about a time when you felt scared. Remember to include the following information:

When did the incident happen?

_____

_____

_____

Where were you?

_____

_____

_____

How did you feel?

_____

_____

What happened?

_____

_____

_____

Illustration © 1988, Barbara Firth.

PHOTOCOPIABLE

SCHOLASTIC
www.scholastic.co.uk

READ & RESPOND: Activities based on *Can't You Sleep, Little Bear?*

SECTION
5

Role plays

● Little Bear couldn't sleep because he was scared of the dark. These children cannot get to sleep. How do you think they are feeling? Cut up and match the cards to show your answer.

	scared
	excited
	cross
	worried

Illustration © 2010, Shelagh McNicolas.

Talk about it

A helping hand

● Make up a short role play based on one of the cards.

A little boy is at the supermarket with his dad. He gets lost. Who helps him? What do they say and do?	**Some children are playing in the playground.** A girl falls over. Who helps her? What do they say and do?
A little girl is in bed trying to sleep. She is scared of the dark. Who helps her? What do they say and do?	**Some friends are playing in the park.** A boy falls off the swing. Who helps him? What do they say and do?
A little girl is at her swimming lesson. She slips and falls in at the deep end. Who helps her? What do they say and do?	**A little boy is on a day out with his nan.** He leaves his favourite toy on the bus. Who helps him? What do they say and do?

Get writing

Night-time

> **Objective:** To make adventurous word and language choices appropriate to the style and purpose of the text.
>
> **What you need:** Examples of acrostic poetry, night-time images (for example, nocturnal animals, the moon, someone sleeping, street lights), an enlarged copy of photocopiable page 28 and a copy for each child, writing materials.

What to do

● Share examples of acrostic poems with the group. Draw attention to how the first letter of each line spells out the word that is the subject of the poem. Explain that you would like the children to write an acrostic poem about NIGHT TIME.

● Read and discuss a variety of night-time stories and poems (for example, *Owl Babies* by Martin Waddell and the poems 'Night-spell' by John Rice and 'Noises in the Night' by Wes Magee).

Identify words and phrases that have been used to describe the night. Discuss their meanings and how effectively they have been used.

● Show the children some night-time images (see above) and ask them to think of interesting words and phrases to describe each image. Record some of the responses on the board.

● In shared writing, explore how the ideas can be fitted onto the simple poetry frame on photocopiable page 28.

● Ask the children to complete photocopiable page 28 independently. Bind the children's poems together to make a class book.

> **Differentiation**
>
> **For older/more confident learners:** Write acrostic poems using other words from the story such as *scared* or *moon*.
>
> **For younger/less confident learners:** Let the children work in a small group with an adult.

The moon

> **Objective:** To draw on knowledge and experience of texts in deciding and planning what and how to write.
>
> **What you need:** Copies of *Can't You Sleep, Little Bear?*, information sources about the moon (for example, non-fiction books, CD-ROMs, video clips, the internet), paper and writing materials.
>
> **Cross-curricular link:** Science.

What to do

● Look at the illustration of Big Bear showing Little Bear the moon near the end of *Can't You Sleep, Little Bear?* Consider the significance of the moon in the story.

● Talk to the children about the differences between fact and fiction. Discuss what the children know about the moon. List these facts on the board.

● Working together, compile a list of questions about the moon that the children would like to be answered, for example: *Why does the moon*

shine at night? How far is the moon from the earth? Why does the moon change shape?

● Demonstrate how to research the answers. Draw attention to the language features of the non-fiction texts (impersonal language, headings, captions and so on).

● In shared writing, demonstrate how to plan, write and illustrate a simple non-chronological report about the moon using some of the information gathered during research.

● Give out paper and writing materials and ask the children to research, write and illustrate their own simple report about the moon.

> **Differentiation**
>
> **For older/more confident learners:** Expect children to use a variety of devices including headings, subheadings and paragraphs to structure the text.
>
> **For younger/less confident learners:** Provide a simple writing frame to help the children structure their reports.

Get writing

What is light?

> **Objective:** To find and use new and interesting words and phrases, including story language.
> **What you need:** Copies of *Can't You Sleep, Little Bear?*, a collection of light sources – objects or pictures (for example, torch, candle, fire), individual whiteboards and pens, photocopiable page 29, writing materials.
> **Cross-curricular link:** Science.

What to do

● Re-read *Can't You Sleep, Little Bear?* and discuss the role that light plays in the story. Identify all the sources of light that appear in the story (fire, sun, moon, stars, lanterns). Using real objects and pictures, explore other sources of light with the children.

● Organise the children into groups of three or four. Let each group choose one of the objects or pictures to consider in more detail. Ask them to compile a list of adjectives that describe the light produced by their chosen light source (for example, stars – shining, twinkling, sparkling).

● Invite each group to read out their adjective list to the rest of the class.

● Hand out copies of photocopiable page 29 for the children to complete, working either individually or with a partner.

● In shared writing, work with the children to turn some of their ideas into a simple list poem entitled 'What is Light?'. For example:

> *What is Light?*
> *Light is a twinkling star.*
> *Light is a burning candle...*

> **Differentiation**
> **For older/more confident learners:** Ask children to write their own 'What is Light?' poem.
> **For younger/less confident learners:** Let children write and illustrate one line for a group 'What is Light?' poem.

Getting ready for bed

> **Objective:** To convey information and ideas in simple non-narrative forms.
> **What you need:** Copies of *Can't You Sleep, Little Bear?*
> **Cross-curricular links:** PSHE, maths.

What to do

● Read *Can't You Sleep, Little Bear?* with the group. Stop at points in the story and encourage the children to recall what happens next, making links to their own experiences where appropriate.

● Look at the second spread of the story where Little Bear goes to bed. Ask the children to speculate how Little Bear got ready for bed. (For example, having a wash, brushing his teeth, looking at a book.)

● Invite several children to describe their own bedtime routine to the rest of the group. Ask them to include information about when and where they go to bed, what activities they do to get ready for bed and who helps them. Encourage the children to describe events in the order in which they occur and to use time connectives (first, next, finally and so on).

● Write the following words on the board: *First, Then, After that, Next* and *Finally*. Ask each child to describe how they think Little Bear gets ready for bed orally to a talking partner and then produce a written recount using the words on the board to frame their recount.

> **Differentiation**
> **For older/more confident learners:** Let children record their ideas in the form of simple numbered instructions.
> **For younger/less confident learners:** Ask children to write about their own bedtime routine.

Get writing

My story

Objective: To sustain form in narrative, including use of person and time.
What you need: Copies of *Can't You Sleep, Little Bear?*, one enlarged copy of photocopiable page 30 and one for each child, writing materials.

What to do

● Read *Can't You Sleep, Little Bear?* Identify the key theme that links the events in the story (Little Bear's fear of the dark) and discuss how this influences what happens in the story.
● Explain that in this lesson you would like the children to plan and write a story about someone who has a fear of something different.
● In shared writing, model how to create a simple story plan. Invite different children to select two main characters, a setting and a story theme from the enlarged copy of photocopiable page 30.

● On a large piece of paper, make brief notes about what is going to happen in the story using ideas suggested by the children. Ask simple prompting questions such as: *When will the story take place? What could be happening at the beginning of the story? Who tries to help the main character overcome their fear? What do they do? How will the story end?*
● Give out copies of photocopiable page 30 and ask the children to plan and write their own stories.

Differentiation
For older/more confident learners: Encourage the children to use description and dialogue to make their story interesting for the reader.
For younger/less confident learners: Provide a simple writing frame or story board to help the children structure their ideas.

Prepositions

Objective: To compose and write simple sentences independently to communicate meaning.
What you need: Copies of *Can't You Sleep, Little Bear?*, a teddy bear, individual whiteboards and pens, paper and writing materials, the children's designs from 'Design a bedroom' page 20 (if completed).
Cross-curricular link: Geography.

What to do

● Look through *Can't You Sleep, Little Bear?* and ask the children to identify all the examples of prepositions (position words) in the text (*by, around, near to, beside, above* and so on). Write the words in a list on the board.
● Ask the children to suggest other words and phrases that describe position. Add these to the list.
● Place a teddy bear in different locations around the classroom. Working in pairs, ask the children to write a sentence on their whiteboard,

describing the position of the bear and using a suitable preposition from the word list. Remind the children to use a capital letter and full stop to punctuate their sentence.
● Invite pairs to read out their sentence. Draw attention to the fact that some prepositions have similar meanings so there will not always be a correct answer.
● Working individually or in pairs, ask the children to write some sentences on paper to describe the bedroom they designed for Little Bear in the 'Design a bedroom' activity (if completed). They should include a position word in each sentence.

Differentiation
For older/more confident learners: Let children use a thesaurus to search for alternative prepositions.
For younger/less confident learners: In guided writing, compose a description of Little Bear's bedroom using a suitable illustration from the book.

Get writing

Night-time

- Use the frame to write your own NIGHT TIME poem.

N _____

I _____

G _____

H _____

T _____

T _____

I _____

M _____

E _____

Illustration © 2010, Shelagh McNicolas.

PHOTOCOPIABLE

SCHOLASTIC
www.scholastic.co.uk

READ & RESPOND: Activities based on *Can't You Sleep, Little Bear?*

What is light?

● Write two interesting words to describe the light produced by each object.

_____

_____

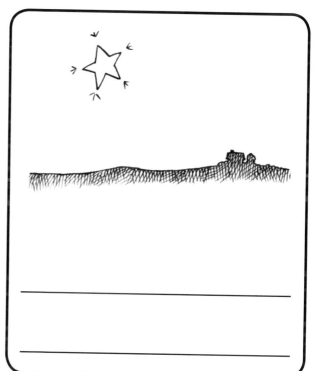

_____

_____

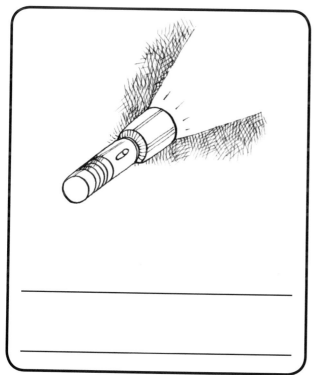

_____

_____

_____

_____

Illustrations © 2010. Shelagh McNicolas.

SCHOLASTIC
www.scholastic.co.uk

PHOTOCOPIABLE

READ & RESPOND: Activities based on *Can't You Sleep, Little Bear?*

My story

● Plan and write your own story about someone who is afraid of something.

Choose two characters.

Choose a setting.

Decide what the main character is scared of.

● Now turn over and make notes about what is going to happen in your story on the back of this sheet.

Illustrations © 2010, Shelagh McNicolas.

PHOTOCOPIABLE

SCHOLASTIC
www.scholastic.co.uk

READ & RESPOND: Activities based on *Can't You Sleep, Little Bear?*

Assessment

Assessment advice

Assessment for learning can take a variety of different forms including observations, discussion and questioning, analysis of children's work, peer- and self-assessment. Children's performance in all of the activities in *Read and Respond: Can't You Sleep, Little Bear?* can be evaluated using one or more of these assessment techniques. Assessment will inform teachers of the level of progress children are making towards achieving specific learning targets, thus enabling you to plan the next steps in learning at an appropriate level. It

may also highlight gaps in teaching and learning which can then be addressed in future lessons.

The activity outlined below provides a framework for assessing the children's ability to speak audibly and with appropriate expression when retelling a well-known story, to recall the main events in a familiar story in the correct order and to use story language (for example dialogue or other words and phrases from the story). Evidence for assessment will be gathered from teacher observations and peer-assessment.

Puppet show

> **Assessment focus:** To show understanding of story themes and structure by retelling the story in an audible voice, sequencing the main events correctly and using phrases from the story (e.g. dialogue).
> **What you need:** Copies of *Can't You Sleep, Little Bear?*, photocopiable page 32 copied onto thin card, scissors, drawing/art materials, sticky tape, small garden canes or lollipop sticks.

What to do

● Read and discuss *Can't You Sleep, Little Bear?*, encouraging the children to recall what comes next at different points in the narrative. Examine the main characters' actions and their consequences to secure the children's understanding of how the main events in the story are connected and build towards the ending.
● Explore the dialogue. Ask the children to identify the repeated phrases spoken by each character, for example, *The dark all around us* (Little Bear) and *Can't you sleep, Little Bear?* (Big Bear) and write these phrases on the board.
● Practise reading out the repeated phrases,

encouraging the children to use suitable expression for each character.
● Explain that in this lesson you would like the children to work in pairs to retell the story using puppets. Emphasise that you would like everyone to remember to speak clearly, to tell the story in the correct order, to use words and phrases from the story and to use different voices for characters. (You may find it helpful to list these marking criteria on the board to help the children to remember them.)
● Give out copies of photocopiable page 32 to each pair. Ask the children to cut out and decorate the bear shapes to create simple puppets to represent the characters in the story.
● Give the children time to plan and rehearse their retelling before presenting it to the rest of the group. During this rehearsal phase, move around the classroom making observations. Talk to each pair about what they are doing and make sure that everyone is contributing to the task.
● Invite each pair to perform their retelling to the class. Ask the rest of the children to listen carefully and respond by commenting constructively on the way the story has been presented.

PAGE
31

READ & RESPOND: Activities based on Can't You Sleep, Little Bear?

Puppet show

● Cut out and decorate the bear outlines then attach sticks to the backs to make them into puppets. Use your puppets to help you retell the story of *Can't You Sleep, Little Bear?*

Illustrations © 2010, Shelagh McNicolas.

PHOTOCOPIABLE

SCHOLASTIC
www.scholastic.co.uk

READ & RESPOND: Activities based on *Can't You Sleep, Little Bear?*